Jesus and the Howling Monster!

Stephen D. Jones

Order this book online at www.trafford.com
or email orders@trafford.com

Most Trafford titles are also available at major online book retailers.

 www.trafford.com

North America & international
toll-free: 844 688 6899 (USA & Canada)
fax: 812 355 4082

Our mission is to efficiently provide the world's finest, most comprehensive book publishing service, enabling every author to experience success. To find out how to publish your book, your way, and have it available worldwide, visit us online at www.trafford.com

Because of the dynamic nature of the Internet, any web addresses or links contained in this book may have changed since publication and may no longer be valid. The views expressed in this work are solely those of the author and do not necessarily reflect the views of the publisher, and the publisher hereby disclaims any responsibility for them.

ISBN: 978-1-6987-1652-7 (sc)
ISBN: 978-1-6987-1653-4 (e)

Library of Congress Control Number: 2024904815

Print information available on the last page.

Trafford rev. 04/02/2024

Dedicated to my three-year-old granddaughter. We were reading a story together and I had no idea it included a monster. Fearing the monster, she became very quiet and could not sleep that night. However, the more she thought about it, she realized on her own that the monster in the story wasn't real. The storybook has become one of her favorites. And I realized that Jesus, too, could be great at taming monsters! To Brielle - and all youngsters who overcome their fears. This is a re-telling of the story of Jesus healing Legion found in Mark 5.1-20 and Luke 8:26-39.

- Stephen Jones

One day, Jesus was traveling in a new land, among a people he did not know. As he walked along, he noticed something surprising. He saw a man attached to a large rock, with chains on both of his wrists. And he was howling, like a wild animal. "Ahh-wooooo! Ahh-woooo!"

There were a few people around who seemed to know him, but they ignored his calls for help.

Jesus didn't ignore people. He asked someone, "Why is this man chained to a rock? Why is he not free?"

His caretaker answered, "He is filled with many voices and we are scared of him. The children won't come near him because they believe he is a howling monster, for he howls like a wolf, like a wild dog!"

Jesus replied, "So he screams and howls and no one helps him? No one comes near him? No one talks to him?"

The man responded, "That's right. We call him Legion because he is filled with so many voices. He scares us."

Jesus asked, "When does he howl?"

The caretaker said, "Only when he is upset."

Jesus said, "I might howl, too, if people chained me to a rock. Why is he upset today?"

The man said, "It's because of you. Someone told him that a prophet was passing by. That is why he is calling out to you, 'What do you want with me, Jesus?' He hopes you can help him."

The caretaker said, "If I were you, I wouldn't get too close."

As Jesus approached, Legion became upset, and he began howling so loudly that his voice echoed across the lake. "Ahh–woooo!" He was a large muscular man, and Jesus was surprised the chains could hold him down.

Jesus came near and said, "What is your name?" He said, "They call me Legion, for I have many voices inside me."

Jesus said, "You are not a monster, are you, Legion?"

Legion laughed, "No, that is just a game I play with the children. It is best that they stay away. I can't always control myself. Children are scared of monsters, so they stay away."

Jesus asked, "Why are you chained here?"

Legion answered, "The townspeople are afraid of me. When I can't control myself, I howl. People are afraid of wolves and wild dogs. So, they chained me here. And a kindly man comes around once a day to feed me. Everyone else leaves me alone."

Jesus asked, "Would you like to be free?"

"Oh, Yes," Legion replied. "I don't want to hurt anyone, but sometimes there are bad voices inside my head."

"So, if I quieted the voices inside your head, and you were free, would you like that?"

"Oh, Jesus, I have dreamed for this! Can you do this?"

Jesus responded, "With the Spirit of God working through me. Do you believe that God can help you?"

Legion said, "Yes, but why would God care about me?"

Jesus said, "God cares about you because you are a child of God. You are as valuable as anyone. Do you believe that?"

Legion said quietly, "I've never believed that. But I suppose God created everyone and everything. And me, too?"

Jesus said, "Yes, Legion, I'm going to pray that all these voices leave you now and forever. And you never have to howl again, like a wild animal. Do you trust me, Legion?"

When anyone talked to Legion, he always looked down.

But sensing Jesus was different, Legion looked directly into Jesus' eyes, and said, "Yes, Lord, I believe in you. I believe you can do what you have said."

Jesus laid his hands on Legion's shoulders. He wasn't used to being touched, and he jerked wildly. But then, he settled down. And Jesus prayed to God for the voices to leave Legion now and forever.

And people who were watching saw something amazing. For the first time, Legion was settled. He was peaceful. He acted like a person, not a monster at all!!

Jesus motioned for the caretaker to unlock his chains. The caretaker was hesitant. Was this just a show? Could the old Legion take over again? Could someone get hurt?

But the caretaker walked over carefully, and slowly unlocked one chain and then the other, and backed quickly away.

Jesus said to the caretaker, "No need to be afraid. For this man is free from his past."

Jesus asked, "What was your birth name, Legion?" He responded, "Phillip."

"Well, Phillip, your faith has healed you this day, and you are free. Take off these tattered clothes and clean yourself up. For you have been cleansed from the inside by God and now you can clean yourself on the outside."

"Go, Phillip, and live your life! And be peaceful to all you meet.

"Oh, and Phillip ...

...no more howling!!"

He turned, and laughed, and replied, "No more Legion!"

Discussion Questions:

Jesus loved everyone. And he wasn't afraid of Legion. Can we love everyone, like Jesus?

What if you met a child with no hair, because the child had lost her hair in a treatment for cancer? Would you be scared of a bald child? Would you be scared of an adult who was your height? Would you be scared of a blind child? Would you be afraid of a child who had lost his legs?

Do you have children in your class or neighborhood who are hard to like? Can you love and accept them as Jesus did with Legion?

Some adults have "voices" inside their heads that confuse them and cause them a lot of pain. Do you ever have differing voices inside you? Is that confusing? What are these voices? What if your mother's voice would tell you not to do something, but your friend's voice tells you to go ahead and do it? How do you listen to differing voices?

Monsters aren't real. You know that, don't you? But we all have things of which we are frightened. What makes you frightened?

Jesus healed people. He healed blind people, and lame people, and deaf people. And he healed people who were frightened or disturbed. The Spirit of Jesus heals people even today. Do you believe that?

Whom do you most easily relate to in this story? Legion? Philip? Jesus? The townspeople? The guardian who fed Legion daily? The children?

This story begins with Legion, who was a very frightened person. And it ends with Legion becoming Philip, a man capable of loving others. Jesus brought about this change. Can you imagine this change happening to someone today?

Jesus said to Legion, "God cares about you because you are a child of God." Are you also a "child of God"?

Stephen has written numerous books, though this is his first children's storybook. His most recent books are *Learning Jesus,* Wipf and Stock, 2021; *and Galusha, Crisis and Courage in a Civil War Pastor,* Trafford Publishing, 2021. He serves as co-pastor of The Beloved Community of First Baptist Church of Kansas City, Missouri.

Bob Holloway is an award-winning illustrator and painter. His favorite mediums are pen-and-ink and mixed media pen-and-ink colored with oil. Bob is "artist in residence" at First Baptist Church. His work can be found at

http://bob-holloway.squarespace.com

Printed in the United States
by Baker & Taylor Publisher Services